Presentation Skills

Portraying Confidence, Answering Tricky Questions & Structuring Content

Table of Contents

Introduction

Working as a director of a UK based training company, I have been designing presentations for over 10 years. The techniques that I will show you in this book are the same techniques that I and my fellow trainers use on a daily basis to design presentations. Our presentations are delivered to audiences of all sizes, from small groups of 2-3 people to large conferences.

A well-structured presentation will have 'flow'. The content will appear logical and relevant to the audience. This will ensure your audience remains engaged and willing to participate.

During my psychology career, it has struck me that a person can improve their presentation style dramatically in a short period of time. They can improve their confidence and reduce nerves with just a few key pointers.

You can choose to read a full length book and try to digest over a 100 pages of content. But as a psychologist I know that you will likely only skim read the content, picking out a few key pointers that ring true to your situation. This book, whilst short, holds all of those key pointers that you would have picked out for yourself.

This book is adapted from a UK training course. You will notice it includes scientific references as the content is based on scientific research. For example, (Othman,N, and Amiruddin, M.H. 2010) refers to the researchers Othman and Amiruddin who conducted scientific studies and published their findings in 2010. At the end of the book you will find a full reference list. This shows the details of the full science paper. Chances are you probably won't want to read these papers, but they are listed, should you wish to.

Many of our readers find it useful to re-read the book from time to time. Your brain will often pick up and remember different key points to last time.

Designing Presentations

Before reading on, you might find it helpful to consider some presentations you have attended in the past. Which presentations captivated you? What did you like about the presentation? What did the presenter do? What did they not do? This short exercise will help to highlight some of the key aspects of successful presentations.

Before you can start planning your presentation, you need to decide its aim. Most presentations aim to inform, instruct, persuade or inspire. Your presentations may have multiple aims. Either way people will be learning something from you. Knowing the aim of your presentation, makes the design process much easier.

The Audience

When designing a presentation, you need to consider your audience in the first instance.

Think of a presentation that you will be delivering in the future. If you do not have a presentation in mind, try to think of a scenario in the future where you may have to present one. Ask yourself the following questions regarding your audience:

Who are they?
Is it their choice to attend?
What do they already know about this subject?
What are their likely attitudes/biases?
Is it possible some individuals might have hidden agendas?
Is their mind already made up?
Would they appreciate a formal or informal style?
What questions might they ask?
What are their expectations of you?
What are their expectations of your presentation? Consider delivery methods, information provided and what they are expecting to leave

with.
Are they expecting to enjoy your presentation?

Strong Beginning, Strong Ending

Presumably, you want to create a lasting impression for your listener. You want them to be able to recall your presentation in the future and remember it favourably. So how do you achieve this?

Primacy & Recency Effect

The beginning and ending of a presentation are the most critical parts. People are most likely to recall either the way that something started (primacy) or the way that something ended (recency) (Palmquist 1979, Yates and Curly 1986, Leventhal 1983).

Make sure that you have a strong start and finish.

The Beginning – The 'Hook'

So how do you begin? Ideally a facilitator/colleague would run through the housekeeping and then introduce you. This would leave you free to open the presentation with the 'hook'. If this is not possible, you would most likely want to do the introductions, housekeeping and then deliver your 'hook'.

The 'hook' needs to be something that will grab your audiences' attention. Here are some example hooks:

Topical Story - A topical story can help bring the presentation into everyday life. As it is familiar to the audience member, it can quickly gain their interest.

Shocking Statement - A shocking statement can make the audience sit up and listen.

Anecdote - An anecdote should be relevant to the subject, brief and, if possible, personal. The willingness to talk personally can make the audience warm to you and feel at ease.

Quotation - Quotations could be from a well-known person or author. They need to be strictly relevant to the topic.

Facts and Statistics - These can be good openers. They should be interesting and ideally surprise the audience.

Mind Reading - If you consider the audience to have preconceived ideas regarding the presentation, you might want to address these as your opening hook. For example, 'If I were a member of the audience, I might be thinking...XYZ'. This type of hook helps the audience feel like the presenter understands them. They are subsequently more likely to actively listen and engage.

As an example, for a presentation called 'Presentation Skills' we might open up with:

'People fear public speaking more than death. Is that really the case? No'. We would then go on to explain that whilst studies have found that when people are asked to specify **common fears** they do specify public speaking more than death. However.....when asked to specify their **top fear**, death is selected most often.

The Ending Statement

You want to create a strong ending to your presentation. You would usually provide a summary and give the opportunity for any questions. Many presentations then fade out after it is established, rather awkwardly, that nobody has any further questions. This is where you can create a strong finish.

Your presentation can end in a variety of ways. You might choose a relevant story, anecdote, interesting fact or dramatic statistic. You might decide to link the 'ending' back to your original hook. Ensure the ending statement is short and succinct.

It is important to maintain eye contact with the audience during the whole of your final statement.

Activity
Spend at least ten minutes thinking of various 'hooks' and 'endings' you could use in your presentation.

Keep in mind your particular audience. Consider what 'hooks' and 'endings' would work best.

Comment
You should now have a few ideas as to how to start and finish your presentation. Remember the start and finish of the presentation are vitally important as primacy and recency effects are influencing people's current, and future, evaluation of your presentation.

It might be that as a result of analysing your audience expectations, you realise that certain beginnings could be more effective than others. For example, if you know the audience are against the ideas that are to be presented, you might choose a mind-reading hook. This would help to lower their defences as they feel you at least understand their point of view.

The Middle

When creating your content there are various aspects you need to keep in mind, such as:

- Structure
- Learning Styles
- Cognitive Load
- Timing

We are now going to look at each of these in turn.

Structure

Structure is incredibly important when designing a presentation. A good structure will help to ensure your presentation flows and makes sense to the audience. It also ensures that you only include relevant information and are not tempted to demonstrate your in-depth knowledge by including everything you know about the subject. As the information is highly structured and links together, you will likely find that the content is also easier to remember.

In addition, having a strong structure makes it easier to cut material out of your presentation at short notice. This can be very useful if you suddenly discover you have less time to deliver your presentation than originally planned.

The diagram on the next page shows how you can structure your presentation.

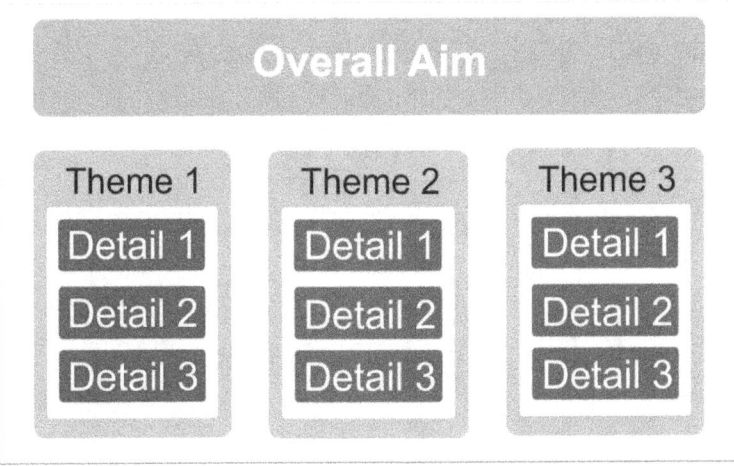

First, decide the aim of the presentation.. What are you hoping to achieve? Next, you decide which three 'themes' best support your aim. Finally, you decide which three 'details' best support your themes. These could include stories, anecdotes, data etc.

Here is an example for a partially completed design for a sales pitch.

You will see that the presentation's content all stems from the aim.

The structure of your presentation can be amended as required. You might find that you want to add extra themes or details, or even remove them. For longer presentations you might need to add 'Subjects' in to your structure.

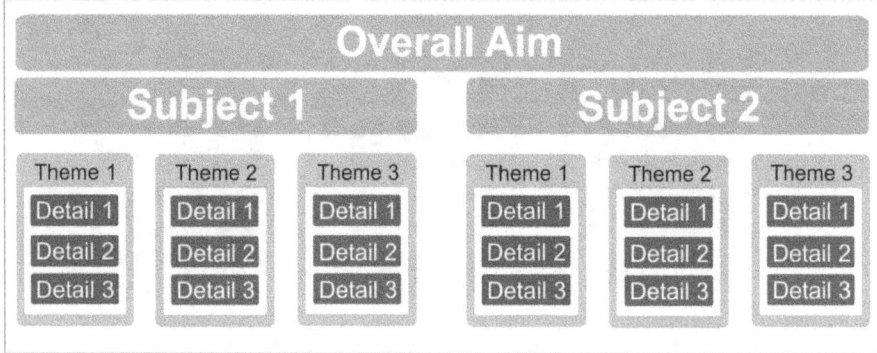

Here is a partly completed version of our 1 Day Presentation Skills Workshop structure:

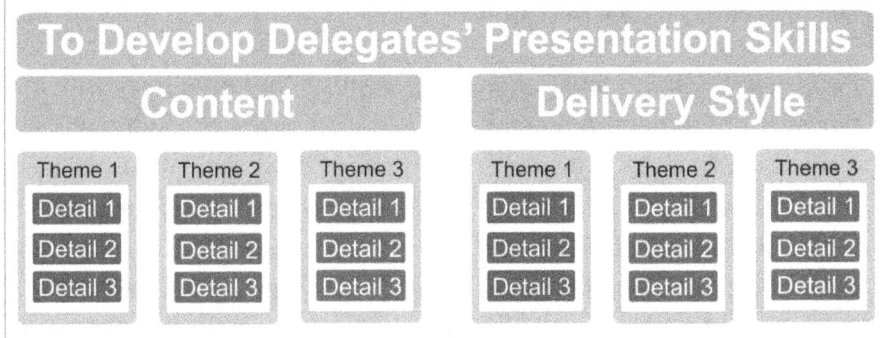

So, now you know how to start your presentation, finish your presentation, and how to structure the main content. The only elements you need to add in are the signposting and the summarising. In general a presentation should:

1. Start with a Hook.

2. Provide the audience with an overview of the content of your presentation. This is often called Signposting. You can talk them through your Subjects and Themes. To add a little interest at this stage, you might decide to add in the odd Detail.

3. Present the content.

4. Summarise the key points. This would include any conclusions you have made.

5. Finish with a strong ending.

Learning Styles

Presentations consist of the presenter delivering information to audience members. The presenter is, in effect, teaching the audience. It is therefore important to understand how people learn in order to ensure your message is delivered successfully. Individuals have a preference for the way information is presented to them, in order for them to process it.

Fleming/Vark's Model of Learning

Fleming and Vark's model of learning suggests there are three different types of learner preference. They are visual, auditory and kinaesthetic/tactile. During a presentation it is likely that audience members will have different learning preferences. In order to appeal to everyone's learning preferences, your presentation should include visual, auditory and kinaesthetic/tactile elements (Othman and Amiruddin 2010). If, for example, a presenter spent a long time just talking, a visual learner may struggle to take in the large amount of auditory information and subsequently lose their concentration.

Visual Learners:

In order to appeal to visual learners try to incorporate some of the following in your presentation:

- Have words written down
- Use pictures to describe things
- Use time lines, flow charts, spidergrams, pie charts etc.
- Write things on a flipchart (this can be done either by you or an audience member)
- Have paper available for the audience to make notes
- Use handouts
- Use presentation slides or OHP's
- Create posters as one of the activities
- Use Videos

Auditory learners:

Presentations naturally lend themselves to auditory learners. In order to further appeal to auditory learners try to incorporate some of these into your presentation:

- Stories, anecdotes and quotes
- Small or large group discussions
- Debates

- Videos with auditory

Kinaesthetic Learners:

In order to appeal to kinaesthetic or tactile learners try to incorporate some of these:

- Hands on activities
- Tasks which involve movement
- Frequent breaks to allow for movement
- Swap groups around to allow for movement
- Role play

Cognitive Load

When designing presentations that aim to provide information or explain concepts to an audience, you need to consider cognitive load. Cognitive load refers to the load placed on the working memory (Sweller 1988).

It refers to the amount of discrete units of information that can be retained and assimilated in short-term memory. People learn best when they can build on what they already know. The more a person has to learn in a short period of time, the greater the load on working memory.

G.A. Miller carried out various studies and found that, in general, we are capable of managing about 7 'chunks' of information in our short-term memory. People can manage 7 'chunks' + or – 2. Some can manage only 5 chunks, whereas others can manage up to 9.

Presenters should ensure their presentation reduces unnecessary load. This is particularly relevant if it is a new concept to the listener, as their working memory will likely be over-stretched. You need to look for ways to reduce cognitive load.

Activity
Create a plan of how you would reduce cognitive load in your presentation.

Comment

There are various ways to reduce cognitive load. For example, a diagram can often be a more effective method of conveying information than providing an auditory account. The visual aid would reduce the cognitive load on the working memory.

Another way to reduce cognitive load is to use 'scaffolding'. This involves introducing a simple idea and gradually increasing its complexity.

Timing Issues

You may decide to write your presentation out in full, later converting it into notes. If you do so, you will be able to estimate how long your presentation will last.

On average 110-120 words can be presented to an audience a minute. For example, if you were requested to present for 20 minutes, you would need about 2200 - 2400 words. Alternatively if you have written 2200 words you can estimate that it will take about 20 minutes. Ensure you allow additional time to answer any questions.

Delivering Presentations

First, recall a few presentations you have previously delivered.What went well? What didn't? What, do you think, are your strengths and weaknesses when delivering presentations?

When we ask this question to our delegates on our training course, the following development areas are often mentioned:

I let my nerves get the better of me.
After the presentation, I realised I had missed out a couple of statements.
I had a person in the audience that made me lose my confidence and I fell to pieces.
I had a person in the group that was rude and I struggled to manage them.
I got asked a few questions that I didn't know the answers to. I am concerned this made me look foolish.

This book will focus on how you can manage and overcome these common scenarios.

Nerves

If your nerves are too intense they can interfere with performance (Tanaka 2006). This is because nervousness can reduce your working memory's capacity (MacLeod and Donnellan 1993). High anxiety states can come from an over-focus on the self. In turn, over-focusing on the self often results in poor performance (Daly et al 1989). You should aim to try to keep your main focus on the environment and the presentation, although I appreciate this can be difficult.

Impression Management

In order to manage your emotions it is useful to understand why you are fearing the situation. A large part of your nerves are likely related to concerns over the way that others will view you. You want to present yourself in the best possible way. It is natural to try to manage the impression that people have of us, hence the title of this section 'Impression Management'. People want to manage these impressions for instrumental and expressive reasons.

Instrumental: We want to influence others and gain rewards (Schlenker 1980).

Expressive: We have an idea of how we want to appear to others. We present ourselves in a way that is consistent with this image. In situations where embarrassment may occur, it threatens this image.

Physical Effects

It is very common for individuals to feel anxious before or during public speaking. The individual may experience a variety of 'symptoms'. These symptoms may differ from one event to the next.

There are many physical effects the body experiences when in a state of anxious arousal. Due to the fact that the body thinks it is in danger, more blood pumps to the muscles in order to prepare it for 'fight of flight'. Blood is taken away from other parts of the body such as the stomach, skin or head. The body sweats more, breathing speeds up and heart rate increases. Throat muscles contract making it more difficult to swallow. These effects result in the many symptoms that anxiety produces. Deep breathing and sipping water can assist in managing the symptoms.

Reducing Nerves

In order to reduce your nerves it is vital you prepare and rehearse your content. If you are happy with the topic and feel that you have great content, that is well rehearsed, you can reduce 75% of your nerves.

Plan the first sentence you intend you say word-for-word and rehearse it. Keep a strong focus on this first sentence. This will help to reduce the negative thoughts that can occur just before a presentation.

De-sensitization can also help to reduce anxiety levels (Kirsch and Henry 1979). Exposing yourself to situations where you have to speak publicly will gradually reduce feelings of anxiety. The natural thing to want to do is to avoid situations that make you anxious. However, if you can face them, you can become desensitized and your nerves will gradually reduce. As a result, delivering a presentation will feel less daunting.

Realise that the anxious feelings will quickly pass. When delegates attend our presentation skills training course, they are incredibly nervous. At the end of the course, delegates report they found their nerves tended to disappear completely after presenting for 5-10 minutes.

Portraying Confidence

Our delegates often ask us how they can portray confidence to the audience, even if they are feeling incredibly nervous. This can be achieved through controlling gestures and actions.

Here are some actions to try to **avoid** when delivering presentations:

- Continually clicking your pen on and off.
- Trying to hide yourself with your clothes e.g. pulling your sleeves down over your hands.
- Persistent itching. Nerves can make people continually scratch their head, arms, legs or the back of their necks.
- Excessive arm movements.
- Rocking backwards and forwards on your feet. This can irritate the audience.
- Crossing your legs whilst standing. This position can make you appear unconfident.

Actions that portray confidence:

- Hand movements that relate to what you are saying. For example, if you have four points, you might count them out subtly on your fingers. If you are referring to opposite sides of an argument, you might gesture either side of you when speaking about the opposing views. If you are making a particular point, you might pinch together your thumb and nearest two fingers. Otherwise a comfortable neutral position for your hands can be maintained.

- Position yourself to further make your points. To explain details you can move towards your audience. When summing up a point, you can step backwards. If you have opposing views to illustrate, you can state one point whilst standing on the right side of the stage and state the other point of view while standing on the left side of the stage. To refer to different points in time you could walk along an imaginary timeline.

- Try to walk about your stage if possible. Walk around the tables as you talk but ensure that people can still see you, you don't want to talk to people's backs. If you are using a u-shape room layout, trying walking into the u-shape. This is particularly good during discussions. When walking about, consider your visual aids such as projector screens.

- Ensure you maintain a confident posture. Consciously drop your shoulders and push them slightly backwards, feet shoulder-width apart and balance on both legs.

- When we are nervous we tend to speak quicker and are more likely to speak in a monotonous tone. Make a conscious effort to speak slower and vary your tone. Speak slower for key points, complex concepts, complex numbers and any emotional content. Speak quicker if you are trying to encourage and motivate. Remember to vary your tone.

- Use pauses of 2-3 seconds to indicate a new topic. You can also use pauses when making key points. If you have a habit of using a filler word such as 'um', try using a pause instead. Filler words usually come at the end of a sentence as we try to think of our next sentence. A short pause will look perfectly natural.

- Connect to your audience with eye contact. Try to give eye contact to everyone in the room. For larger audiences ensure you make eye contact with different sections of the audience. Eye contact should last for 2-3 seconds. Be careful not to focus too much on one particular audience member, it could make them feel uncomfortable. Eye contact not only portrays confidence, it enables you to monitor how your audience is receiving your presentation.

Ideally you would practise the above techniques prior to delivering your next presentation. It can be difficult to see ourselves as others see us. To overcome this, try videoing yourself. It can be a great tool when polishing your presentation style and will help you to manage your nerves. Before delegates attend our presentation skills workshop, we encourage them to video themselves delivering a presentation to friends or colleagues. When they view the videos back, many are surprised at how they appear. We often hear delegates say '*I didn't realise I looked down at my notes so much*' *or* '*I had no idea I spoke so fast.*' Videoing yourself can provide a real insight into how to improve your presentation style and portray confidence to your audience. Another common comment is '*I was surprised at how confident I came across, I felt really nervous.*' This is great and gives the individual a real confidence boost, reducing nerves dramatically.

Difficult People

Having a challenging person in the audience can be a real hindrance to your presentation. If you don't have the tools to manage it, they can knock your confidence and affect the rest of the group. People who are difficult are often trying to meet some unfulfilled need (Cartwright and Cooper1997).

They may:

- Enjoy social interactions and feel the need to be the centre of attention.
- Feel insecure and try to cover up their insecurities by displaying their expert knowledge.
- Want people to admire them.

Activity

The four following behaviours are often displayed by audience members:

Behaviour One: Regularly talks to the person next to them in hushed tones.

Behaviour Two: Likes to talk at length in front of the group. Likes being the centre of attention and has many personal experiences they wish to share. Their contributions are often lengthy which puts time pressure on your presentation. They can also irritate other audience members who have come to listen to you, not this individual.

Behaviour Three: Wishes to demonstrate the fact they are knowledgeable on the subject. They might quote names, articles, research, facts and figures. They challenge the presenter or give additional information to the audience.

Behaviour Four: Tries to trip you up. They might say things like, 'How would you know? What experience do you have of doing my job?'

For each behaviour try to identify the underlying need. What are they hoping to achieve? What do they want? Keep your notes for the next activity.

Activity

Use your notes from the previous activity and design strategies on how you think it might be best to deal with each behaviour type.

Comment

Here are some strategies. You might have come up with others.

Behaviour One: Regularly talks to the person next to them in hushed tones.

Strategy: Through your actions, you ideally want to remind them that they need to be listening to you. While talking to the rest of the group position yourself near them. This helps you to exert your presence and make them feel uncomfortable enough to stop their side conversation.

Make direct eye contact with them. If there are activities, split the group up so they are not working with the person they continue to speak with.

Behaviour Two: Likes to talk at length in front of the group. Likes being the centre of the group and has many personal experiences they wish to share. Their contributions are often lengthy which puts time pressure on your presentation. They can also irritate other audience members who have come to listen to you, not this individual.

Strategy: Politely interrupt. 'That's an interesting point you just made. Let me stop you there and get the views of the rest of the group.' If the person is going off topic, you could say 'that's an interesting point, we are struggling a bit for time at the moment but maybe you and I could discuss it when we break for tea and coffee?' Once the person pauses, try to involve the rest of the group by asking the group a relevant question, for example 'What key factors do you think were at play in this situation?' These techniques will help you to limit the amount of time this individual takes up during the presentation. You can use their desire for attention to your advantage, for example, you can ask this person to assist you should you need a volunteer for a particular task.

Behaviour Three: Wishes to demonstrate the fact they are knowledgeable on the subject. They might quote names, articles, research, facts and figures. They challenge the presenter or give additional information to the audience.

Strategy: If they mention something that is relevant and could be helpful to the rest of the group, thank them for their contribution. On occasion you may even encourage them to carry on speaking. Ask them where they found the fact/article/research. This will firstly help you to establish whether it was from a reliable source and if it was, you could either research it in the break or encourage your audience to look it up after the presentation. It could even add value to your presentation and provide an interesting alternative perspective. If you disagree, rather than disagreeing openly, you could ask the other listeners what they think in order to create a discussion. Do not try to put them on the spot. Using these strategies can help to meet the individual's desire to receive recognition.

Behaviour Four: Tries to trip you up. They might say things like, 'How would you know? What experience do you have of doing my job?'

Strategy: Agree with them. You could say 'you are right, I have no direct experience of doing your job, however....'

If you are having a disagreement with a delegate, suggest that due to time constraints it might be better to leave the discussion there for now and move on with the presentation. 'Shall we agree to disagree for now, so we can move on with the presentation? I am happy for you and I to continue the discussion in the break.'

This person may have a hidden agenda. They may be trying to prevent the success of changes in the workplace. They might also be acting disruptively because it was not their decision to attend your presentation. It might be that a manager has asked them to attend and they would rather be working through their to-do list. In this situation, it can help to acknowledge that they may have been asked to attend the course by their managers and it might not be what they would ideally chose to be doing with their day. This understanding can help to reduce some of their reluctance as they at least feel you understand their position. You can then move on with your presentation. Often once they have expressed their thoughts, they are happy to engage with the material.

Language That Creates Positive Interactions

The type of language you use during your presentation can impact the level of positive rapport you develop with your audience. Good manners are, of course, very important. Here are some positive words and phrases that can also help.

1. General Phrases

Have you considered?
Would you mind?
What do you think?
I am sorry that you feel that way.

2. Phrases For When You Disagree

Instead of using the phrase, *'you are wrong'* or *'that is incorrect'* you could replace this with *'I can see where you are coming from'* or *'I see why you would think that'.* This implies you believe the person to be competent and it reduces their feelings of embarrassment for providing the wrong answer.

3. Phrases To Use Instead Of The Word 'But'

Yes and ………………
However…………..
Yet…………

Memory

Many presenters fear they will forget elements of their presentation. We often hear people say 'By reading directly from my notes, I made sure I included everything in my presentation. It also helped with my nerves, although I want to appear more natural in future' and 'I'm worried I'll forget what I need to say'. There are various tips to help aid memory.

- Memorise your first two lines, word for word. This will help you start the presentation in a confident manner.
- Memorise your last two lines. This ensures a strong finish.
- Use notes. Most professional presenters will refer to their notes occasionally. If you use postcards, tie them together. This way if you drop them, they will still be in the correct order.
- Try creating an A4 visual map of your presentation. You can create a diagram of how your presentation is structured. This is covered in more detail in the designing presentations section of

this book. A Spidergram can work well in this situation. If you use a web search engine and type in 'Spidergram' you will see various images and sites detailing how to create a Spidergram. Many people find that remembering a Spidergram is easier than remembering pages full of written notes. This is because people can often recall visual representations easier. As a Spidergram usually consists of only one page, you can also have it in front of you in case you need a prompt.

- Obviously, practice is key. Try to practice your presentation at least a few times.

Managing the Question and Answer Section

Many presenters fear they will be asked a question they do not know the answer to. One thing to bear in mind, is that no audience can expect you to know absolutely everything about your subject.

Activity
What strategies could you use if you did not know the answer to a question? Have you used any strategies in the past that have worked well?

Comment
There are various strategies you can use when you don't know the answer to a question. The most popular and effective amongst experienced presenters are:

- Offer an educated guess or opinion, say as such, and give your reasons.
- Offer to get back to them once you have researched the answer.
- Ask the rest of the group what they think.

You might want to set the rules about questions at the start of the presentation. You could either state that you are happy to receive questions during the presentation or you could mention that you would prefer to answer questions at the end of the presentation. When delivering our workshops, some of our presenters find that if they accept questions during the presentation, it can easily take them off topic. If questions are asked frequently, it can really impact on timings and flow. If an audience member asks them a question they will say something along the lines of 'That's a really interesting question. I'll pop that on the flipchart and we'll come to that in the Question and Answer section at the end of this section/presentation.'

It is a good idea to decide before your presentation how you will answer questions. Will you answer them as you go along and in the question and answer section at the end, or will just answer them in the question and answer section at the end? Make the decision in advance and make sure you stick to it throughout the presentation for any lengthy questions.

References

Cartwright, S. and Cooper, C.L (1997). Managing Workplace Stress. Sage.

Daly, J.A., Vangelisti, A.L. and Lawrence, S.G. (1989). Self-focused Attention and Public Speaking Anxiety.

Kirsch,I. And Henry, D. (1979). Self-desensitization and Meditation in the Reduction of Public Speaking Anxiety. Journal of Consulting and Clinical Psychology, Vol. 47, Issue 3, pp. 536-541.

Leventhal, L., Turcotte, S.J., Abrami, P.C. and Perry, R.P. (1983). Primacy/Recency Effects in Student Ratings of Instruction: A Reinterpretation of Gain-loss Effects. Journal of Educational Psychology, Vol 75, Issue 5, pp. 692-704.

MacLeod,C. and Donnellan, A.M. (1993). Individual Differences in Anxiety and the Restriction of Working Memory Capacity. Personality and Individual Differences, Vol. 15, Issue 2, pp. 163-173.

Othman, N. and Amiruddin, M.H. (2010). Different Perspectives of Learning Styles from VARK Model. Procedia – Social and Behavioural Sciences, Vol. 7, pp. 652-650.

Palmquist, W.J. (1979). Formal Operational Reasoning and the Primacy Effect in Impression Formation. Developmental Psychology, Vol.15, Issue 2, pp.185-189.

Tanaka, A., Takehara,T. and Yamauchi, H. (2006). Achievement Goals in a Presentation Task: Performance Expectancy, Achievement Goals, State Anxiety, and Task Performance. Learning and Individual Differences, Vol.16, Issue 2.

Sweller, J. (1988). "Cognitive load during problem solving: Effects on learning". *Cognitive Science* **12** (2): 257–285.

Yates, J.K. and Curley, S.P. (1986). Contingency Judgment: Primacy Effects and Attention Decrement. Acta Psychologica, Vol 62, Issue 3, pp. 293 - 302.

More books by this author

How to Manage Teams: The No Waffle Guide to Managing Your Team Effectively

Change Management for Managers: The No Waffle Guide to Managing Change in the Workplace

How to Manage People: The No Waffle Guide to Managing Performance, Change and Stress in the Workplace

How to Manage Stress in the Workplace: The No Waffle Guide for Managers (EBook Only)

Manager's Guide to Providing Feedback: The No Waffle Guide to Providing Feedback and Rewards (EBook Only)

Coaching Skills for Managers: The No Waffle Guide to Getting the Best from Your Team (EBook Only)

What Other Marketing Books Won't Tell You: A Brutally Honest Account of Marketing a Small Business

The Counselling Sessions: Overcoming Feelings of Irritability and Anger in Relationships

The Counselling Sessions: Overcoming Anxiety and Panic Attacks

The Counselling Sessions: Overcoming Low Mood and Depression

www.ingramcontent.com/pod-product-compliance
Lightning Source LLC
Chambersburg PA
CBHW070759180526
45168CB00004B/1677